W9-AYG-286

Fall 2004

I want to be a Builder

I WANT TO BE A
Builder

DAN LIEBMAN

FIREFLY BOOKS

A FIREFLY BOOK

Published by Firefly Books Ltd. 2003

Copyright © 2003 Firefly Books Ltd.

All rights reserved. No part of this publication may be reproduced, stored in a retrieval system or transmitted in any form or by any means, electronic, mechanical, photocopying, recording or otherwise, without the written permission of the Publisher.

First Printing

**Publisher Cataloging-in-Publication Data (U.S.)
(Library of Congress Standards)**

Liebman, Dan.
   I want to be a builder/ Dan Liebman. —1st ed.
[24] p. : col. photos. ; cm. (I want to be)
Summary: Photographs and easy-to-read text describe the job of a builder.
ISBN 1-55297-758-7
ISBN 1-55297-757-9 (pbk.)
1. Building trades – Vocational guidance – Juvenile literature. (1. Building trades – Vocational guidance. 2. Vocational guidance.) I. Title. II. Series.
624/.023 21   TH159.L54 2003

Published in the United States in 2003 by
Firefly Books (U.S.) Inc.
P.O. Box 1338, Ellicott Station
Buffalo, New York, USA., 14205

**National Library of Canada Cataloguing in
Publication Data**

Liebman, Daniel
   I want to be a builder / Dan Liebman.

ISBN 1-55297-758-7 (bound)
ISBN 1-55297-757-9 (pbk.)

1. Building – Vocational guidance – Juvenile literature.
I. Title.

TH159.L53 2003   624'.023   C2003-902828-3

Published in Canada in 2003 by
Firefly Books Ltd.
3680 Victoria Park Avenue
Toronto, Ontario, Canada, M2H 3K1

Photo Credits

© Al Harvey/Slide Farm, pages 8, 15, 17
© Laura Zito, page 9
© MediaFocus International, LLC, pages 10, 11
© PhotoDisc/Ryan McVay, page 12, front cover
© Mark E. Gibson Stock Photography, page 21,
© B. Allan Mackie, page 23
© George Walker/Firefly Books, pages 5, 6–7, 13,
   14, 16, 18, 19, 20, 22, 24, back cover

The author and publisher would like to thank:

Morah Duclos
Massimo Ighani
Trevor Trottier
Dylan Walker
Nicholas Walker

Design by Interrobang Graphic Design Inc.
Printed and bound in Canada by Friesens, Altona, Manitoba

The Publisher acknowledges the financial support of the Government of Canada through the Book Publishing Industry Development Program for its publishing activities.

Builders like putting things together.

They build houses, apartment buildings and office buildings.

Some builders work high above the ground.

And some builders build ships.

This builder drives a loader. A loader is a machine that moves a lot of soil quickly.

When you start construction, you dig a deep hole. This hole is called the foundation.

head protection

foot protection

MUST BE WORN

All builders must be very careful and pay attention to safety signs. They wear helmets and safety boots.

Builders hang their tools from their belts.

Builders need to be strong to do heavy work.

It's a long way up! That's why builders use ladders and lifts.

Every member of the building team has an important job to do.

This carpenter works with wood.

Builders learn their skills in school and on the job. Apprentice builders earn money while they learn.

Building a log house requires special skills. These men are putting up the roof.

Being a builder is hard work. These builders are very proud of the job they do.